I'm 17 and out of
of
My Mind

ISBN-13: 978-0-9842626-5-6
ISBN-10: 0-9842626-5-2

First printing, October 2010

Cover photo furnished by Matt McGill

Published by:

ThomasMax Publishing
P.O. Box 250054
Atlanta, GA 30325
404-794-6588
www.thomasmax.com

I'm 17 and
out of my Mind

100 poems
by Matt McGill

ThomasMax

Your Publisher
For The 21st Century

Table of Contents

*This book is dedicated
to all those that I truly care for
and care for me.
Those of you know exactly
who you are.*

"MY FIRST STREAM OF CONSCIOUS"

Dance they cried under the naked sun,

   We are all mad but sensitive

Seize the day,

   Divinity is on its way

   Find the key,

Open the unknown

Step inside to see me,

Along the road I never did say,

   Beautiful day once did come,

   Misunderstood is my game look beyond the
reality wave,

Stop inside someone said,

   And I died alone only to be reborn.

5-11-10

"CLUB NIGHT"

Serious Attitude

On the way,

Cologne smell pulls people,

Redbull and Beer

Is our favorite drink,

Ripped Jeans

Tight shirt

Jelled hair

Fire in my pants,

Welcome to Club Night.

5-13-10

"JOGGING"

Running,

I slip on my special shoes

Bathing suit
Tank top
I-pod tucked in,

Motivational fast pace sounds pushing my legs forward,

Run all through the city,

I want to stop but I can't,
I won't
The music gets louder

Heart beats faster,
Time slows down

The Animal inside me comes out to sing,

Voices of past calling me lazy, a loser

Bind me to the ground, I will not stop I will break through

Breathing heavier thoughts to stop get stronger

I see the light no need to quit

I am Immortal..... Powerful!!!

No... I'm just jogging.

"A question"

I have a question,

It's not hard to ask,

Just a simple question from me to you

Just a few little words I'll say to you

No need to worry, erase all fear

This question I have is something real, something special

Misunderstood is my vessel

Climb aboard…. live life anew,

Have you guessed my question yet?

It is not why?   Or some bullshit philosophy,

It's very simple

Just think it through,
What's the question?

Have you guessed it yet?

"Jersey Shore Trash"

As I gaze out into the sea,

> I hear annoying sounds piercing right through me

I for some reason wish I was gone,

> Is it the people I'm with or the place I'm at….

Drugs, Alcohol, Sex, Cigarettes,

> The people I'm with are against all four,

The current keeps pulling,
> The boats keep on sailing,

Poseidon would be angry at how we treat his gate,

> Oh Well,

It's what we do we are not special I promise,

> Look at the human race from another point of view,

A creature of the forest perhaps,
> We are ugly,

Let's take a ride down the shoreline,
> Go for a swim

And party on the sands of ignorance.

Explanation
"I wrote this while at Point Pleasant Beach NJ."

"COYOTE SPIRIT"

Laughter,
        I am the Coyote
                Within my soul
  Great wisdom I constantly grab,
            I see myself in the mirror

    Only to return to a world of mystical power...
Beauty...
      Mystery...
           Strength....
              Use your strength
Go forward beyond the light,
          I am the coyote,

Travel desert, valley, hills, air, water,
               Nothing can stop me
   This is all mine......I pilot my fate
What am I?   Praise
      This spirit guides me,

    All praise the Coyote.

"DREAMING A GODDESS"

Smiling lady at my thighs,

So Beautiful
Like love at first sight,
Blonde short hair,
Her soft tan skin,
I haven't seen you before I wish you were here,
I wish you were real,
But we all awake in one way,

A spirit of compassion and beauty has contacted me
What a day but night,
You are my one and only love for this
night.
—I am conscious dream —
Ruler of the night,
When your mind seems right
A message from where?

I want to know!
I want to know where?!
Please! I ask
Please take me there

Explanation

"I had a dream where I was in a library with a beautiful girl laying on my lap. Once I made eye contact with her I felt unbelievable unconditional love and fell into her eyes."

"THE FIGHT"

Courage, you may pass

If you're scared get out of my way,

I walked down the road,

Stop and stare into the sky,

Heart beat racing,

Mind drifting,

Sky darkened,

I start to laugh,

Smile.

I command myself,

I'm walking to the cabin alone

The ground makes a noise,

Heart beats faster

Mind floats into itself,

The sounds of a beast hiss behind you,

Turn around,

Total blackness,

Something attacks you.

Claws your face to feet,

– Survival –

Are you more insane?

5-10-10

"CONSCIOUS CHANGE"

What is happening?

I really do not know,

Changes,

A monster of energy

Thrust forward,

Prosperity,

A few little helpers carry me away,

Into my destiny,

I'm choosing my destiny,

It's a good one,

Oh I promise…

It's a good one.

4-10-10

"DIMITRI'S PARADISE"

Don't be scared my friend you have nothing to fear
                     This experience is filled with love,
Now we fire it up,

       Off we go into a forgotten paradise,

         What is happening I can not say

I love this amazing thing, Sounds of space move all through me,

      – I am floating in a web –

 Why can't it last forever?
                       I'm in a heavenly bubble of love
Without you it's just me,

I see the world in a whole new way,

            Colors floating all around

Hearing strange voices coming from the lights,
             What is it that I've just seen?

         I'm afraid we're running low my friend.

Oh no. Please no.
    We love you so much you'll be back again soon

So long friends I love you too.

      What the fuck just happened man.

Words are not our tools we don't need them, they don't work.

        We experienced the portal through Dimitri.

6-11-10

"WEIRDO'S"

People are weird,

They keep up with their weird values
Weird morals,
Weird beliefs,

How lovers behave is completely weird,

People's religions are weird,

A person's curiosity is weird,

School is weird,
Business is weird,
Money is weird,
Appearance is weird,

Our death,
birth,
Being in the moment,

Are all aspects of being weird,

Nothing can oppose our weird will,

We are naturally weird,

We will always be weird.

Accept it.
You and I

Are fucking strange.

7-2-10

"OUR GAME"

I was fortunate enough to see the time pass before my eyes,

Breath in - Breath out

Moments of pure serenity,

Breath in - Breath out

Clear truth,

As I dance on through chaos

Breath in - Breath out

Have I reached it?
Gone, the truth has disappeared,

Thanks for playing you may start over at any time,
No memory

It is a game without an end,

The most fun of all is your control of the game,

Decisions,
Actions

Breath in - Breath out

Keep playing my friend.

5-18-10

"SAVING MYSELF"

Don't be afraid it's only me,

 Not some stranger
                              On a unknown island

Looking for you

    Oh please, please be...
                        Silent!

You haven't a clue

The preacher is died no one to lead,

Ok... that's perfectly fine

          -I will heal myself-
                          -I am powerful-
But a number,

          What is truth?   Haha stupid question,

When it's coming I see it first,
                        Decide a path

      Conscious thinking will save me.

Explanation

"The phrase "conscious thinking will save me," you will see in a few poems I wrote. The reason behind the phase is that it is a mantra, which I would say anytime I had a fear of death. I fought the fear of final destination; this was one of my weapons."

5-18-10

"SHOWER"

All hail the water goddess of day and night,

　　Drenches me,
　　　　　　Warms me,
　　　　　　　　Loves me,
To hot,
　　To cold,

　　Blood will calm to a slow stream at her power,

Have you ever tired the waterfall?
　　　　　　　　Ears plugged?
　　　　　　　　　　Eyes shut?

For a moment you'll experience real peace,

　　Then the awareness of the peace,

　　Then the peace is gone,
　　　　　　　　Was peace ever there?

　　　　-Allusion-

I send the water goddess my graces,

　　For I am clean and renewed,

　　　　Every time I become

　　　　　　One

　　　　　　with

　　　　　　You.

5-18-10

"SHUT UP!

Screaming voices in my head

    Souls wanting out,

        Sometimes I can't understand the voice,

        Sometimes it's a well-spoken demon,

      Other times it's a fun-loving spirit that just laughs,

Brings a smile to my face,

        -I am the King-

Stay away,

      I'm not afraid to sin,

Haha sin?

    Sin is a joke,

       You are a joke,

If you won't leave

I will kill you,

        Go to someone else's brain.

    Not Mine!   Not Mine!   Not Mine!

I am way to powerful for you,

        I challenge you,

You're already died,

Goodnight I'm off to bed...

      For good.

    DIE VOICE!!!

5-11-10

"THINKING WITH YOUR DICK"

Thoughts only on her,

Do anything to feel good
Oh so good,

Give me a chance baby,

I'll make good lovin' out of you,

If you walk away my friend will be very upset,

Don't wanna cry,
I'll do anything!

-Pathetic-

Why is the little man in charge?

-Pathetic-

Stand up to him

-Pathetic-
I can't...
You Can't!

Pathetic so fucking Pathetic,

Sexuality is all alone.

You are useless, Selfish, an asshole,

Relax pleasure man,
Relax.

7-5-10

"CALL ME"

The strange creature with a driving sexual desire,

Stay back.

Imagining the thoughts disgust me....

Later that day,

Attack another fear.

Slipped a pretty one my number,

A future lover?

Who's to tell?

I promise though,

I will find out soon enough,

Though all those torturous voices,

I hear an Angel...

Pushing me to do it,

Do it,

Do it!

I grabbed her pen and a napkin,

Handed them back as one,

I wonder what I did with that.

She smiled goodbye,

Then later a hello.

Explanation

"I wrote this after I gave a beautiful girl my phone number at a local coffee shop."

"SMOKED DREAM"

I call myself a psychonaut on a journey to discover me,

　　　　Reality's a wave　　　I'm drifting away,

　Has my voyage just begun?

　Has insanity taken over me?
　　　　　　　Later I found it's only stage one.

Feeling this fucking guy around,
　　　　　Mocking, Mocking.

　　Next some say is impossible to describe,

　　Recall a daydream is hard on my mind.

　　Going from a crib to a separate place,
　　　　　　　Brain Fuck,
Head straight up burns my soul

Slanted left than slanted right,
　　　　　Electrical line cooled my mind.

Line swimmers and water slippers showing me there ways,

　　　After that I can not recall.

　It was like a dream,

　　　　Other dimensional without a doubt in my eyes,

Is it another step closer to discovering me?

　　　Only if I am the *God of Insanity*.

7-6-10

"RESPONSIBILITY OF YOURSELF"

The world by the balls,

You can have,
Do,
Be anything you like.

Work hard

Creativity

Break through walls

Your dream is there to transform.

Stay formless,

Responsibility of yourself

- KEY -

Empowerment is a river it must always flow.

Find your passion,

Fuel it,
Work even harder

Be well,

And you will be given your dream...

"MONEY"

This paper moves, controls, changes people.

Unpredictable currency chaos,

Beautiful

Greedy

A love, hate relationship,
It builds but crashes lives.

The Green Monster is here,

Jump along or he'll kill you.

Companions and friends seem died when the Green Monsters around,

I want to grab him by the throat,

Put a collar around his rough dry neck,

And make the beast my pet.

I have no fear
Only a dream,

Where the green Monster see's me

Immunity is my game

Fantasies are reality

Green Monster is my Bitch...

My little, little Bitch.

3-27-10

"SHIFTING MYTHS"

Dionysus

Gave us the key

Gave us insanity

Insanity is a pathway,
             Pathway towards truth,
                          Bliss

        Play the fool,
                 I want to be the fool.

   Dancing down the road – Smile please

  Understanding yourself is an act of courage,

             Sacrifice is needed,
I gave my mind.

   If I'm free will I survive,
                 Can I survive?

"Give me blood," says the voices.

        When it's over I cry…

  Only to be lifted into a joyful realm,

     When it's gonna be alright.

5-13-10

"SIGNS"

Weight limit 4 tons,

  Speed limit 15,

    Riding prohibited bikes on foot walk,

      Bridge weight limit 4 tons,

        Weight limit strictly enforced,

        Bridge may be slippery,

        Motor vehicles only,

          Horses not permitted on bridge,

      Strange town to older town

    bridge to cross the big old river.

"I AM MAD"

I can't see,

I look so deep and so wide,

Without a scope   I don't understand why,

I need you know more than ever,
          Please help me be free
It's all I need
          It's all I want.

No one gets me except for me,
                    But it doesn't matter.

We're all aspects of divinity,

Without mind the universe is placid.

Through the valley we will walk,

Nevermore to be seen the same

-Mystery-

Another step closer,

Difficultly understanding,

Connection is died,

I am Mad.

"AFFIRMATION"

Power

I love empowerment

Give it a try

Only fear the fear

Go after it... overcome it

You are powerful

Keep going... extraordinary feeling

Strength

I am loving,

I am beautiful,

I am evolving,

I am unlimited

Evolving can be controlled if you understand your mind,

Look inside from time to time,

Believe,

Always believe,

Especially in yourself.

5-12-10

"A CREATURE WE TEND TO HATE"

My floor is constantly changing....

Every minute is a new show,

Like a never ending live movie.

The people tend to hate me sometimes

Other times they don't care.

I'm useless to them,
Garbage,
Just garbage.

Sometimes I fly into my floor
And it's a new glorious breezy space

Sometimes rain slides across my floor,

Where I can almost touch it but,
I'm still dry.

I feel movement I stay still,
Fly away,
But will always return.
Humans hate me

Fly on a window.

6-2-10

"SWEET SOULS WHISPER"

I am laughing… Always laughing,

Love it…. I love it so much.

Please sweet soul kiss my neck of eternity as I drive into a successful paradise.

The wall pictures are moving and floating all around,

As if I was watching a movie of horror,

Of mystery.

I step out of the doorway… float over the cliff.

I am one with the clouds,

Still laughing.

You're a minor,

The doctors will not see you.

Really?!

I laugh,

Laugh and keep on laughing.

Make my forehead glow with a kiss from Sweet Soul.

4-8-10

"STICK MAN"

Who's the stick man that I've seen,

Walking so slowly looking at me,

Are you talking to me?

I haven't a clue.

Where did you come from?

Have you always been here?

I'm sorry I can't understand… please forgive me

I see you exist on a dimensional realm made out of light.

Are you my friend?

I saw you walking left to right,
Is that up to down,
Or back to forward,
Upside down to right side up?

You are very interesting… stick man.

You look like a skeleton,

Who's the swimming fish head?

He swim straight through me, was I flying forward?

Oh well,

Farewell my friend,

Farewell.

"COMBINED CONSCIOUS"

I HAD A DREAM LAST NIGHT, FROM WHICH I AWOKE

I ASKED THE MAN,

"WHAT IS IT LIKE TO BE IN MY

DREAM?"

HE SIMPLY LOOKED AT ME

–TERRIFYING–

SPEAKING IN TONGUE

MISUNDERSTOOD

WHAT A BEAUTIFUL JOURNEY,

AND A REMARKABLE THING TO BE SUNG.

I'VE CLIMBED THE MOUNTAIN, TO LATE TO COME BACK

IF I FALL I DIE

BUT I WILL RISE TO ACHIEVE MY POWER,

IT'S JUST A DREAM,

IS IT?

Explanation

"I wrote this after I had a lucid dream. In the dream I asked an unknown man what it was like to be in a dream, due to an inspiration from a scene in "Waking Life.""

5-4-10

"RESISTING SLEEP"

I feel so tired… I feel so sick,

Mixed up chemical's in my head,

The two hours of sleep filled an epical dream.

I can't remember it,

Am I getting lazy?

Or am I just tired?

Am I both?

That's it… No more,

No more laziness!

I want success!

I will do everything with my heart, mind, and spirit.

Do everything I have to achieve something great.

Something real,

Something beautiful.

No one but myself can stop me.

I can't be stopped

Won't be stopped

I am Immortal

A God

With a part time vessel.

5-4-10

"DANGEROUS SHADOW"

I HAD A FRIEND,

WHO TOLD ME AN UNUSUAL STATEMENT.

MOST WILL SAY HE IS INSANE,

FEW WILL PRAISE HIM,

SOME WILL SAY IT DOESN'T MATTER AT ALL.

IS THAT SCARY?

IS THAT EXCITING?

BUT AS FOR ME IT'S ALL TO DULL.

QUANTITY FUELS

QUALITY IS DIED

HIS STATEMENT WAS SPIT INTO THE GROUND.

5-14-10

"WE ARE SO SMALL"

Saturn spurs up

A strong vivid vortex

Pulls energy,

Light,
Matter into it.

I hear an eight dimension is about to emerge,

Ignition of fire furiously spreads

Throughout the chaos

The ice on Pluto remains the same

Mysterious era in deep space.

"The Killer"

The killer is awake with a coffee,

        About to go to work

He sees his wife in the kitchen,

        Sexual thoughts...

    8 hours in... home to sleep.

Outside he see's an unknown black creature,

    Closer... Closer

        Boom! The door is kicked in

The runs upstairs to protect his wife,

        Grabs his smooth dark desert eagle

The black creature steps on the stairs,
        1...2...3...4...5...6...
    Bang! Bang!

    Smoke pours out of the killer's gun...

The sound of a woman's cry torn the wallpaper apart,

    The creature mask is taken off

        Faint

Swallows the gun,

        Makes a loud sound,

 For the black creature in-fact,

        Killed himself.

6-11-10

"HERO VS. FEAR"

The hero enters the purification stage.

After personal death,

He will leave clean,
Strong,
Wise and Brave.

"Stay away,"
The weak one cries,

I have an intense visitation of fear,

I guess you can say.

A challenge has sprung

The hero will be judged

Save us...

WEAK!

Stand up!

Fight!

Become immortal

Be the hero,

Save yourself

That is my lost fear...

"WHINING HIPSTER"

Release the guilt... Preview of freedom

Becoming Lucid... Expression of freedom

Travel the world... Self Freedom

Expand your mind... Freedom from linear thought

Absent of worry... tranquil freedom

Psychonaut... mysterious mental freedom

I want to be free... Set me free

I am completely alone

You're all out there... but next to me?

Can you cry alone?

Is this a lie...? Who's the liar?

Freedom from religion... Who will save us?

Save my Soul

Magical power... mystical freedom

Planned out patterns concern my life,

Seek your path... whatever it may be

Give me the life I've always wanted

I wish you were here to say goodbye... your work is left

What is the color of the waterfall?

Will you be with me to seek the color?
Adventure... Freedom?

Do I have rights...? Is that a freedom? A privilege?

Is freedom the knowledge of no freedom?

Is it just the pursuit of Freedom?

No Freedom

No Freedom at all.

From,

A know-it-all hipster

3-5-10

"POSSESSED"

It was like a dream,

    The connection was clear

                        The evil entered as I
watched

I must have acted completely insane,

                The memory is unpleasant
     Scars are left
                    Burns are seen
     How can one do such a thing?

    A shaman with no direction insight

              Spirits take over
As I watch,
       Trapped in my own mind
The next day had come to find an old man,

Pushed me through
I want that channel died

                 I want to be free

    The night was carved, *"END DREAM"*

Matt McGill

"HPPD"

As I gaze out into the pale blackness
                    Static

    Shapes moving

                              Lights glowing

    As I look straight through another's eye

  Background moves
                          Personality's seemingly
change

                    I'm scared of my mind
          Work,
                    A helpful distraction
     Abstinence

  A war with your head

    The toughest fight

                    To overcome.

6-29-10

"Sacrifice"

I gave up a habit,

I gave up a philosophy,

I gave up darkness,
                    That empowered my eyes.
I gave up that life,

I gave up Facebook,

I gave up some friends,
                    Even some jobs

To touch the skin of all my dreams,

I gave up an attitude,

I gave up a personality,

I gave up a vision,
                    Through the eyes of insanity

        For a vision beyond

My conscious soul,
                    Sacrifice is a friend

        A friend that will

Hurt you,
        Love you,
                Amend you,
                        Change you,
                                Build you,
Give up the sacrifice,

            Give up the man.

7-2-10

"YOU DON'T KNOW SHIT"

I'm a hipster… I protest stupid shit

    I'm a hipster

"I'm not a conformist,"

        Favorite statement

    I know everything

   You're wrong, I'm right

    Cause I'm a hipster

If I can't see,
        I'm going to wear giant black glasses

Sandals of choice… Same Jesus wore

   Smoke pot everyday,
        Go against the system
   Cause I'm a hipster

   You lazy college know-it-all scumbag hypocrites piss me off,

 I get sick at your fucking site…
        Peace, love, no war, no evil
    -Pussy-

Never been in a fight before,

      Piece of shit Hipsters.

"A FRIEND YOU NEVER MEET"

I followed his movements,

    Every step by step

        Slowly merging personalities,

He is my idol,
    But also my prodigy,

This man I speak of you probably never have met

    This guy is a follower,
        Acting exactly like me,

    What a weak personality

        For he needs me,

I'm not a savior or an escape

    I'm just anew you,
        Created through imagination
An interesting way to be born,

    I think my soul has quit.

Ride the twin headed dragon

        Through the flames of your Enemies.

5-21-10

"Mystic Energy"

Morning Awoke

A massive burst of energy

If the energy that shot me up is inside...
Do I have the power to use it?

Send it in any direction I choose?

Sitting underneath the soft whispers coming...
Off the trees,

Laid beside me

Moist wet grass,
Thank you morning dew

Mushroom hunt

A mystic journey in itself

Finds you back with nature,
In nature,
Apart of nature,

You are one with nature

Just don't fool yourself again.

5-20-10

"A CALMED LiGHT MUST GLOW"

A calmed light must glow,

    A mirror is proof of another world

I enter into these other places,
        Everything looks exactly the same
  Only I have changed.

    Quantum leaping,
        Whatever that may be

 Ride along the wind into a paved path,
           Or

    Build a plane and fly all the way to the sky.

I will talk to several of my future selves.

    Advice here... Maybe I'll go there

      Destiny is a choice
  Dig up the fear,
      Fill in the power

Everything and anything you've ever wanted is coming,

     Just look

    It's almost here.

Explanation

"*A calmed light must glow* is an anagram for my full name, *Matthew Douglas McGill.*"

5-16-10

"Mind Tool"

I had an invention once,

Something special,

                Something powerful,

Unlock the unconscious

Channel it through

I walked along some trees,

             With laugh spilling off them,

Mysterious Creatures

I sense a mockery,

          As clouds fly by

An evil vicious fire in the priest's eyes

I've always had more fun
      On these sunny bright modern days,

I'm finished with what I've been told

Now it's my turn

Don't Give in.

6-30-10

"I have a little green"

Going into the world,

One side of the family,

Heritage pride

Separate tradition

Green everywhere,

Parade,

Intense Irish joy... soft peace music

Only enjoyed at times,
Keep a distant

Creation of a safe nest,

Amazing feeling at a time of great stress,

Peace clover sounds,
Moving through me

To be blossomed out in a handsome manner.

What a world to be apart of me.

GREEN IRISH BLUES

"BROKEN ANCHOR"

What a strange terrifying unique experience to undergo.

I was lost

How?

Where?

Who?

All came about

A tiny map and a dot,

Got me safe,

But I anchored on fear,

Making it harder to sail on

ATTACK!

I will attack it

Fearlessness

Great relief when I was told not to drive

RAIN

We are all good... no problems... heading home

That motherfucking anchor won't break free,

I'll have to break it myself... hoping I won't drown.

6-4-10

"Jungle... Please NO Thugs"

These people must leave

-Arrogant-

I go for a drink,

These bacteria waste pop-up in my sight

All hail the God of War

For you hide within everyone

I hold the power to ignite you... set you loose

Maybe I'll bleed

When was the last time you picked up a book?

A time to read or gave a hand to feed,

Fuck You!

If you die no surprise,

Why if you kill you're a hero,

a man of respect,

Stay the fuck away...

Rules Fade

It's Jungle Time

Who's playing the LION?

5-13-10

"THE DIRECTOR"

Since the day we awoke

This dream has been a Zoo,

My reality is moving

When my life slows down,

             It becomes a show

When it changes,

         It becomes a movie

I'll make sure my show is a comedy,

I'll make sure my movie is an epic masterpiece.

5-27-10

"I HATE THE WORD DEEP"

A BREADED MAN IN THE CENTER OF THE CROSSROADS,

A SEARCH FOR KNOWLEDGE,
                    LITERATURE WILL PROVIDE.

THE THINGS WE'LL DO FOR MONEY,
                    SEEM TRIVIAL

   INSULTING TO OUR VERY OWN IMAGINATION,

BUT... IT'S WHAT WE WANT AND EVEN NEED,

  AS LONG AS A LESSON IS THERE AND IN A FUN-LOVING,

        ATMOSPHERE,

   RECORDING THE VOICES IN MY HEAD

ASPECTS OF MYSELF...? HIGHER SELF...?

OR... IS IT COMING FROM SOMEWHERE ELSE?

        DEEP!

   WOW MAN THAT'S FUCKING DEEP,

PUSSY POEMS BY PUSSY PEOPLE

        STAY BACK I SAY

         WRITER'S TRUTH IS ALMOST HERE

AND I ROLL DOWN A VALLEY LAUGHING,
                    CONSTANTLY LAUGHING

      FREE FROM FEAR.

5-14-10

"PROM"

I fell so nervous,   I can't understand why

      I drive up,

Nice to meet you... picture here,

            Pictures everywhere

    Off we go... awkward Aura,

I've been away for so long,

         One's hot... one's cold

It was a rainy evening.

        Speeds nearly 90mph

   how will I ever get home

Now we're here... lets get out and have some fun

     I am all alone

A familiar face brightens up my state... time to dance

   No thanks, we ate but all this is just not for me...

Grabbed my jacket its time to go,

         Goodbye old friends

As I walked out the door,

       Never to be seen again.

Explanation

"This was written after an experience at a prom I was invited too, which was not my thing. I was there for an hour than left."

6-1-10

"Angry Water"

RAIN

A powerful force drenches me all the way down to the ground.

Open the Ground

Jump in the Hole

Maybe some presents on the other side

Where we're going I haven't a clue.

Poems about love

Piss me off.

I want to bury those thoughts and burn

The lakes of

uncertainty,

Let me be Free

Stop now...

The music gets louder... much, much louder

But the rain slows into a gazed color filled day

Burn my misery away,

Fly Away.

5-9-10

"SATAN'S RIVER"

I walked down the path on an august dawn,
                 The river split in two
Water is fire… Morning star arose,
The Devil said, "Come with me, I'll make you an immortal man."
"No I'm fine with being me not some entity,"
            The Devil boiled the water in fury
For he wanted my soul,
            I hear the cry of an old man asking, "Why?"
"Not the young boy's soul."

Immediately I awoke… "It was just a dream,"
               Satan whispered in my ear,
Go away demon you can't have my soul.
             "Let's make a chance on a flip,"
"DEAL," the Devil yelled.

So I said, "Heads you're died, and Tails I'll see you nevermore,"

     Coin is thrown… Satan has been tricked

     Too late

     Cheers back to hell,

Since that August day,
           The Devil I have not seen

     Immortality I feel all throughout me

     There's a light… it's in your heart

Morning Star is in plain sight… When it's dark

     You know the Devil is died.

6-10-10

"Job under pressure"

Some Business people are cocksuckers

    Let's be real

I've seen them,
        Worked under them

      BULLSHIT...
               Patience gained
   Stress levels hitting peak

    Blood pressure up

    Adrenaline kicks in

    Energy... Ready to go

    -DEFENSE-

Run... Just go run...
           Don't stop

    I am Immortal

Break,
     Keep running
On,
      Run away
  Through,

   I have a bridge I would like to show you.

"ARRESTED"

Today is just another day,

I feel I have lost my mind,
                    I feel I have gone insane.

        Is this really happening?

Please don't be true,
                    I'm in the woods with no one around.

This is my TV screen,

My eyes see from the past,
                    Familiar figures in every sight

        When the vibrations erupted in a chaos of fury,

        I lost control   I lost my head,

        Give me pain!
                            Pain!   Pain!   Pain!

        Pain is a friend... relieve emotions

Will I be O.K.?
                    Someone tell me I'm not a bad person

I want to be told that I am not evil.
                Am I loved?   Love is all I want...

            But I still keep crying alone.

Explanation

"This was written after I was arrested in the woods with 3 friends for smoking pot, and drinking alcohol."

3-29-10

"My Darkness"

Demon!
Leave me now
Fascination keeps you around

Mystery of you gives you power

Look down... Cure
Look up... Goodbye head
Nothing matters,
Nothing is good,
People are a disease,
Your life has no meaning,
DIE DEMON!
You are powerless

The light I hold is more powerful then you

I will fight you
I will taste blood
I will kill you
Be gone evil spirit

Your fate is death!

4-14-10

"Backyard Meditation"

The dog is connected,

      I see the woods as my screen,

               Lens adjusted

I've seen it through the end,

       My birth, my Death, my Dream

       Attunement REIKI

Focus on the dog,

        All else disappears

I feel as if I am one of them,

             Crave a forest walk

If I am there I'll be anew,

          Me and you

    Why does the grass grow?

       -Unknown-

So beautiful,

       When you slow it down, focus in

     Music is loud... motivating... exotic...

     Am I crazy?

   No... I'm just sitting alone.

5-14-10

"Lover's Lust"

Open your eyes as I say,

Have you seen this pale green plant?

   Beautiful fine sunny day

I want to go outside... dig a hole perhaps

   Stuck inside a prison chasing paper to get by

   Her soft smooth pale skin... a chance... touch it

Five months later...

                     Touch it baby touch it,

Come on baby, me, and you... one

      I want to see through you, not just be inside

So join me I say and we'll take our dreams away,

      Fly with me... away... away

I want you by my side,

                  So no worries baby

Come along for the ride

            As we become one every single night.

5-17-10

"Highway Man"

Welcome highway man,
>Follow me

Bright spinning, glowing, pulsating lights

>Again?

Puts the hat on before he walks to the door,

History up and down racing throughout my mind… split second

Strolls on over… how are you doing today?
>Papers all set

Then he said a question…
>I could get smart, lie, or truth,

Do you… know why I stopped you?

So I answered very calm, respectful, and confident

Speed… going to fast,
>My father is one of you,

Embarrassment, no more

Once more I am just me, not my daddy's prodigy

The sickening stomach less fear is an evil power,

Stay away… Stay away

Farewell Highway Man.

5-25-10

"Crazy Vet"

Resist,
          I want to drift back into sleep.
  I won't
          Stay awake! Stay awake!

    The voice in my head shouts,
                    Let's drive
Familiar places show me familiar faces.
                    Wait...

There was a gust of darkness that casted over me last night,

          How long did my dream last?
Drive goal,
          I see it in plain sight

I wonder who was here questioning what is real, no clue

Sitting outside... breakfast,
                    Veteran from Vietnam

    Strolls over dressed for combat

    Mind to be institutionalized

That goofy, limped, ignorant, happy,
                    Loving, hating,

                    Mother fucking vet.

5-31-10

"Sunset Moon"

Is it jealousy?

                Pathetic

I feel scared,

          The closer someone comes to acting like me

I hate it!   *Why?*   *I love it!*

        Fucking go away

This strange emotion arose,

            The ground unfolds

      Mystery enters

I can't avoid it,

          Conscious of what's happening

    I don't know myself

I thought I did until I entered the trance,

            Evils hand

Pushed the swing,

        Until sweet soul laughed me away,

A sea of simple joy⋯

       Until I meet a lover⋯

Until I walked straight through divine moments of truth,

Until I got angry at that Sunset Moon.

6-18-10

"Acid Mind"

I stare out into the vast planes of the universe,

Those without this experience,

Feel it is a wondrous place to gaze beyond,

While in reality it is solely a place to rest,

As my eyes and mind do a flip.

Staring at myself

Insanity is scary

False beliefs,
            Beauty

I Survived

Controlling the game is the most fun of all.

"Something from work"

I can barely breathe,
                  Anything to get me through

The creature is lounged... relax man relax

Deserve all the treats we have special for you
                           Take them,

I have nothing to blame only a grip on responsibility

        Flashing lights... Go away,
            A time, a place to be enjoyed

        It's fleeting my friend,

Times a healing shore

        Life is set... ride the wave

Scream them away,
             You scream they're running scared

        It's all in your fucking head

Stay happy friends,
      I closed the door to something that wasn't there

 New door... new era

These days seem long with a lust for a girl with good luck,

      Let the channels flow through me.

"BIKING NEW HOPE"

I want something new.

A bike ride through a strange town will fuck justice.

    Old man sitting by the river,
            Shouting across the cannel
Fishing polls facing forward,

        COLD!
I feel sick,
    This shade is not for me.

Enter the calm town,
    My eyes in disguise behind big round sunglasses

Along my path, stopped by a duck,
      A constant disarrangement of luck

Peeled an orange next to a waterfall,
        River man with cigar
Kayaks up river,
    A thinker I rode past,

    Back to good old New Hope

Explanation

"I wrote this after a bike ride along the Delaware river. "New Hope" is a small artsy town along the river; it was the most important place to me at the age of 17. My friends and I actually started a small holiday on Tuesdays in titled, "New Hope Tuesday." Every week we would meet in town and spend the evening with good talks, good walks, good tobacco, and good food. We always had a memorable time on "New Hope Tuesday."

"Lost Somewhere"

Creation is a driving force.

Bringing us all closer to a star

They shine so bright,

                        I will swim
though them.

      This sparkled black ocean

           Drowned me

Over and over before eyes will change
color

        Personalities come

        -Confused-

Lost in the chaos of ourselves

        Pierce the next reality

Free from past history and fear…

       My name is…?

10-31-09

"MY FIRST TIME"

I took the brown and the white

This small paper what an impact on my life

Laughter upstairs waiting for something to appear

I want the hot tub to relax thinking on my life

The bear distant in the woods as I turn to see the floor glowing forms

Keep the joy flowing

Will this ever end?

I'm all alone with no one to help me see

I can't believe all that I've seen

I want to tell the world to have my first time

When I knew what was going... This is new

So powerful I can't believe it's true

Reality with a new light

Why end now no need to fight

How you feel is the experience

Avoid the media it's usually a lie

Go to yourself and have a fun time.

"ATTACK FEARS"

I am afraid
But I'm coming

I might have a fear,
But I'll walk on through

-Courage-

Transcend and mistrust any constant flow

Step on ground

Believe

You are everything

Don't be scared,
Never live in fear

Are you fucking serious?
Scared?
Scared of what?

Don't quit

Believe

Strong uplifting force from beyond

Power off... Doubt

Stab the heart of fear

Mind Warrior
Save your Kingdom!

5-11-10

"Restaurant... Silent Killer"

In the moment

-Stress-

"Get back to work!"

"Boss"

"Yes?!"

"I want to kill you"

Silence is key

Keep those thoughts in your head,

A few hours later you'll wish he wasn't died

Don't get lost in the anger... quick moment

Because your boss...

Might want to kill you too

But only at that moment

Pretty soon it's all gone

We're learning

-Patience-

7-2-10

"INVISIBLE FORCE"

A concentration of power

Will take me through,
                    Break through

All my aspects of fear

A guided energy on a massive scale

I am channeled

The 7 pipes will pour on site,
                    At my command

I will command and demand

The release of this energy

Make me fly.

6-20-10

"Monster Man"

The pain burns my head

Go away

I'm always crying

I feel sore,

Keep going

Run... Run... Run

I can't stop,
Nothing to go back too

Only roads ahead

I am over the fear of final destination

Make me stronger

I chased an experience

Several at that,
The joy is the chase

All new... All fresh

Mind in Pain

With a thought comes a feeling,
A monster,

Comes a man.

5-7-10

"Visitations of the Snake"

Snakes are coming,

       A shift is near.

    I have an animal or two inside me

     Which one empowers me?

One snake is here,
       I want a ride

                              –

Fearlessness-
Face the fear,
      Brief the freedom

    Struggle for the top,

Coyote come back,

  More will be waiting

                Just step inside
and see
Snake in the stream,
     What a cool current life.

4-6-10

"Hyperspace"

The buzzing loud sound of being shot forward

Moved me,
Connected me

What I've seen is nearly impossible to describe

Patterns,
Moving... pulling... talking

Skeleton like creature please show me your way

I'm awake I say,
Look at me

I am the universal life force

I am power

I experienced real fear which excites me on every level

I want more!
Please show me more

I love this place... this strange, strange place

The Sci-fi sounds explored my brain

I love hyperspace,
I want to visit again soon

I was catapulted in and brought right back

Joyful and Sad

I can't understand why
Let me stay longer I say,

When the grim reaper comes I smile and say

Take me away.

"LOST IN SELF"

Walk through the desert,

Not wondering where I've been

Just acting a person

Whoever that might be

Stopping here, and there seeing a light through the devils eye

An oasis is at the corner of the sun,

Mythology... Fun

I told a story once to an unknown creature's son

Terror... shot through

I come, baring gifts of sand made out of gold

Read this book friend

You're my friend?

Follow or I'll make you disappear

Walk the sands of freedom barefoot,

No plan...

5-14-10

"Crime West"

We are outlaws

Ride the horse breeze into new land

Our brother

I will not listen,
I don't like rules

Limited horizon... Fuck no.

Mistrust,
Independence

My game

I ride,
I will die as a criminal

-Outlaw-

This is the life for me

Look into my eyes,
Do it
I fucking dare you.

5-16-10

"Policeman in shorts"

The man of law,

Blue shorts,

White shirt tucked in,

High white socks,

Black shoes,

Guns and gadgets on his belt

Clean cut hair with a sharp blue hat

Face,

Business,

Anger,

He takes his job serious

Ladies a Gentlemen this town is much safer

Paranoid

We have fear

Save us

Please... Man of Law please...

Nice Outfit.

5-25-10

"Crazy Stories"

A man came into my day,
Only to be overheard,
He said,
What a beautiful day it is,
It's days like this that makes me happy to be alive.
Beauty,
Absorb it... Soak it
I want to be crazy
Go wild
Anew experience?
I want to share,
All we are is our stories we have to share
I want to change a life,
I want to whiten the shadows of darkness,
I want to go out of my head,
Light
Jumping out of a plane seems interesting for me,
So come on
Nothing to fear
Are you a pussy?
Go wild
I want to be crazy.

"BLIND ATTACK"

The eye is here to stare,
                   Awake the killer

        Fear your fear

Take a knife… use it

                As the killer sleeps
Loud fast heartbeat

         Water hits ground

       Taken away

       Running away

Next thing I here is something strong yet very silent

        "Come with me I have a show for you"

        Terrifying cry

   As my eyes are torn out,
                I'm set free

      Every second alive is an unpleasant, torturous time,

              So long.

5-26-10

"Evolving"

I think I remember that face... 5 years

I feel a glow as I drop a lemon in my drink

Quitting my old habits,
Commitment

I am fucking sick of past regrets

Pussy

They're now a blessing with a mythological mask

Rip the space

An animal noise I love to make,
Its coming

The sound of a shamanic drum,
Beating faster and faster

Hit it once... makes me twitch

Hit it twice... makes me dance

Beat the hell out of it,
Faster, faster, harder, harder

Thrown in a trance

What new things do you have for me?

Make them special,
Make a turn.

"River on Heroes Eye"

Stop staring at me,
Look away!

Gazing at people

Reasoning is died

It seems to be hysterical... I can't stop laughing

"DIRT" is written up against the wall

Who wrote it?
A wise-ass shitty kid perhaps,
But we love him for that,

May the water always be at your eye sight

In a dream that won't last

Stay back,
I am an animal

I will not stop until I kill you

Wake up nigger

You'll die young not even aware

Don't fucking stare at me... look over there!

He wants to fight,

To win is to be completely and totally,

Insane.

6-2-10

"DREAMING HEAD"

I see myself in many ways,
           I pick my own,
                      Trust me I do
I float across into a new found current···
                      Here I am again
Eliminate the air,
          Eliminate the matter,
                    Be gone time
for you are just an Allusion,
               Merge with the Divine
               Beautiful visions
               Eternity of hope
  I have a dream,
          Rope it to yourself
      Blast off
      Follow it,
          As it will follow you
Dogs want to fuck,
         As dreamers do too
I am not alive
I am not died
           Conscious divine
           Beautiful,

  I am a beautiful dreamer who holds a secret power

Open the gates of infinity through the bars made of fear.

4-14-10

"SELKIE"

She is my lover by day,

I love her in every way

By night she is gone

Where did she go?

I haven't a clue,

She loves the water

Maybe she went for a swim,

This time she is gone forever,

Please!

Don't be true

I love a Selkie

Saw a face then later a fin.

5-5-10

"Pre-Vision Quest"

Chewing,
     Time is so slow
          The taste is so bad
Bitter burn,
      Can only be tried
   I want to spit it out... Can't swallow
     Why is concentration so hard?
It's now 7 minutes away,
         Vision quest is near
I'm on a mission,
        Where I'm going I haven't a clue,
To find a fairy, God, any entity beyond this dimension
  Almost here... 3 minutes
           The taste is so distracting
1 minute away,
        Incense lit... time to spit
Vision quest is here,

     Don't lead me astray.

Explanation

"This poem was written while I had a mouth full of
Salvia Divinorum, which was used along with shamanic
drumming music to push my mind into a trance."

5-5-10

"VISION QUEST"

Fly forward

Body is numb

Out of myself,
> What is happening?

A bear singing next to a fire

Snakes staring at me in the face of terror

Opening the Channel

Doorway

Come inside... please come inside

I awoke a shadow person
> I knew real fear

Use your power,
> I laughed

Show no fear

I awoke,
> A hero to myself

Safe journey

It was fun while I was there,

Ancient Central America painted my brain.

5-26-10

"SEA MONK"

What is it like to live beneath the waves?

We try to answer this strange question,

-Sea Monk-

Wise one of the waters,
A god in our sight for he has past
tales,
No interviews

Wait I have a question or two,
He is gone
Vast current,
Wind of the sea... a constant breeze

Boil is fire,
Talk to me please

Speak... bubbles rise

Sea Monk come back,

Meet me in France

Jump on land,

I guess it's only a tale.

"Coyote Walker"

Walks through the city,

Grasp myself

Embracing the beauty

Melting at the misery,

Truth... Connection

Metro ride is smooth

Everyday's not for me

Why care

Shouting at the sky,

I can't scream that loud

With a goblins eye on me

Go away

Laughter is my game

With no joke to be seen

People will never forget my name,

I am Coyote Walker.

6-15-10

"Observing Hors"

The mumbling complaints of the two sitting next to me,

Inhale··· Exhale   release the pain
          Calm me down,
                  Calm me down
Now there three, two sit, one stand,
      All fucking hot, would any of you be up for a bang?
     Do you like my hair cut short momma?
              Latin lovers drifting along
Those fucking hors and cunts disgust me
My nice old friend sat down besides me
        Ripped the beauty of these hors away,
    I wish I saw a smile, not today

     You will end up marring a woman just like your mom,
                It usually happens,
   Those drunken lovers annoy me,
            Let them have there fun
I like this girl, I really do
        She'll be gone soon

     A clear vision··· Fucking all night
The sounds of her screaming an experience into my head.

"Forest & Immortality"

As I walked,

Straight through though the shadow

Of a strange Demon's eye.

I become Immortal

The fight is hard but my will,

Will not subside

The grasses split through an invisible passing.

Walk on brave soul

You will be tested very tensely

If you stumble along,

The trees, Sky, Clouds

Fly by

All eyes on you

Be the King

Chaos through this forest day,

Makes the trees sing.

6-11-10

"Go away Zombie"

For here or to go?

Would you like salt with that?

Have a nice day.

Hi, How are you?

Is it going to rain today?

Will it be busy?

How was your day off?

You make me fucking sick!

Real moments... Died

I guess,

Why?   Is it to hard?

To Scary?

Are you to lazy?

-Repetitive Zombie-

Mediocre satisfaction

My dreams are real,

I will stab the heart of mediocre existence.

Conformity die

Creativity is on our side

Ride the beast.

6-17-10

"SICK HEAD"

I walk the grass,
                  Pick the spores
Makes me sick,
          Why would I when I said I was done

          Pocket full of potential keepers
We all tend to take
             Consciousness
                  For granted
It wasn't until those brief moments of insanity,

          I Survived
    The greatest battle,
              Mind at stake
    Angelic realm... Heal me now
Voices,
      Oh those voices
             Terrifying

   An invisible claw

I will cut off the paw.

7-5-10

"Bad vibe Fight"

Paranoia

Past memories of being screamed

Into a dark trance.

Be Zen

Aloof

Calm yourself

Nervous,
Scared,
Thinking is hard

When I get home will it all begin once again?

Be Zen... Please

I can't go back there,

Relax

Control yourself

Man your emotional storm

Be conscious of the paranoia nightmare.

"Michael"

I was all alone

Can I be saved?

A war with myself,
　　　　　A feeling of dying

　　Mantra!　　　　Mantra!

Conscious thinking will save me, turns into

　　Michael has saved me.
　　　　　　　　Who is Michael?
　　　　　　Angel?
　　　　　　Spirit?
　　　　　　　　　　God?

　　　　　Me?

　At the gates of blurred tunnel lights

　　　　A screamers head came a healers hand
Dream,
　　　　Pain fought... in sight

　　Survival head... I must be

Explanation

"I once had a remarkable experience when I was going through a fear phase of final destination. So this experience started with me lying on my bed shaken in fear, and everything turned white, everything. And a voice came along, pronounced itself as Michael. This Michael told me that I am killing myself, and to start building love on top of love."

5-27-10

"LITTLE MAN"

I feel kind of bad for my little man,

Lonely... ignored

Time to let him shine

A pagan spell will do it justice

For an average man

Little man is king

Humanity is a slave at the power and pleasure

Not for me... I've keep him prisoner

Bars... Blue Aero Jeans

It's time to set him free,

-Go wild-

He's under my order,

My command

Come out become a stiffer man.

You and I we'll drive into a pleasure paradise,

The wheel at a conscious command.

6-29-10

"Fast forward"

Music is helping to cure

Trust in time

Time will heal the conflict in my head

I trust myself

I love myself

This musical shift is a trust into another conscious state,

Vision of hope

Drifting

Forced Back

You will stay!

I love myself

I trust myself

Patience

I can't speed the time

Smile

Times waiting for you.

"Lust an old friend"

Pain... no love

Come to me
                    Be fast

        I'm coming to get you

On the road,
                    My turn to drive

        3,000 miles to success

        Baby I'm here for the ride

You seem much happier seen you've won that prize

        Meet on this special day,

            Together we'll explore
                            -Sexual desire-

    Take you away to a place of
                            Orgasms,
                    Screams,
        And Sweat.

    But,
        I'll take my time

            Talking & talking

            Love me Baby

        Do you know who loves you?

7-19-10

"Drink up"

I hate my job

Alcohol,
　　　　　　　Forget the job
Drink beer,
　　　　Swallow the poison whole

Drown yourself

Drain your mind of all hope

More alcohol

I'm out of control and I don't care at all

Alcohol's a friend?

Consumption on a massive scale,

Our race is drunk,
　　　　　　　　Our people are fucked up
Yes!
　　　Our people are very fucked up

　　　　　　　　Something is very wrong,
Depression... more alcohol

Anger... Large doses of dehydrating liquid

Pleasure vehicle philosophy... everyday is a drunken day

You fucks!
　　　　Keep on drinking your life away.

6-13-10

"Following Words"

Open your eyes on an astral grassland,
    Step into the forest,
                Follow the creation
Path,
        Go farther and farther
All of a sudden,
          A creature crosses
Lead into the forest,
        Deeper and deeper
Enter the cave,
       Can you imagine how it looks?

See the water... swim with the creature
    Leave the cave,
          Run back to the grassland
Float to the sky,
       Open your eyes

Thanks for visiting your imagination,

You may stop by at any time.

5-16-10

"*Sane friend, Sane Isolation*"

I have frustration throughout my dream,

               Show me what I want.

      A new close friend

        All alone

Keep falling down as long as you never hit ground

       Fly by,
           Grab the sun

     Take it into our garden of guilt

        Powerful

   A prophet
        Or a Monster

      Possible both

    I am not insane I promise

    Stay away from this man

     Save yourself

    Maybe a little insane.

7-17-10

"Attracting a Lover"

Cast me... spell

Forceful push towards my soul mate

Lovers Lust

Excitement... once again a kid

We all can use it

Command yourself

Make a call... listen

Here comes the asshole doubt

Why walk in fear?

Watch your lover can be anywhere,
                              Right here?

Massive vibrations

Drawing us closer until our lips almost touch

          Remarkable feeling
Resist,
          Longer you resist... the greater the passion... Connect

This is not lust it is a beautiful bond,

Well,
          There's still a little Lust.

7-21-10

"Tunnel Within"

Fly forward... enter in anew

Beautiful lights,
Pulsations

Losing your minds... the sacrifice

Be a fighter... Stand ground... Be the bridge

Keep the conscious stream clean,
Remarkable discoveries
-New perception-

Explanations seem to roll down the halls of institutions,

The pressure is very intense... The rush is an extraordinary high

The mystery never ends, chasing the limit beyond our capacity

Sad,
Why can't we go there... we will... in time

For now our psychonaut's are left insane, institutionalized, a big laugh,

Or a small rip in a desperate time to swim through an ocean of hope.

5-13-10

"Empower Experience"

As I see all the different walks of life,

They each have a different story,
                              Different experience

Way of life

So who's to judge,
                    We're all one of them too

We are all unique for what we have been through

Continues amazement

I want to know more

Experience is fire...
                    Burn the words

We try to share

We can't connect

Our words are nothing...
                    They're died.

Preview

Become the fire and torch yourself

Believe me

Torch yourself.

5-20-10

"My fun Spirit"

Sweet soul is in my brain,

Swimming and jumping all around

Makes me smile... Makes me laugh

I love Sweet Soul,
On a beautiful day I asked the spirits

"What is your name?!"

Along came a giggling one, he pronounced himself as Sweet Soul

God of laughter... Childish-like behavior and fighter of the demons at night

Conscious thinking will save me

As I write sitting at work... "I will survive"

I start over right now

I made my decision... Now!

As my fear dies my life is arise,
So much ahead no turning back

Save me Sweet Soul... Save me

For I will survive,
My tea read "I am unlimited"

Explanation
"Sweet Soul is a spirit I channeled, during an interesting time in my life."

7-23-10

"Lady by the Waterfall"

Lady by the waterfall,

Wondrous sight to see

Endless beauty,
A mystical mystery

A lady staring down at the water below

Moments of intense sexual power

The moon is always just right…
On these painted nights

The lady will come in many shapes,
Please don't fall

Our sexual mystic bride will be caught

Carried away,
Brought home

Making love while thinking on the waterfall,

The best sound in the world is hearing her moan.

A favorite image stored in the head

A doorway towards my soul mates world

Were she lies down on her soft silk bed.

6-15-10

"Blessing in Disguise"

Changing,
>   You would make me mad even a little sad.

>   Blessing in Disguise

Open up your eyes... More!
>   Dreams are real and I'm coming

The man that throw my mind into a destructive labyrinth

>   Unconditional Love

>   I fought threw it... Never quit

>   The pain is gone in this terrifying connection

I am so damn grateful for all that you've done,
>   You saved me

You scared me... I am a man
>   Weakness... not for me

A little screaming mixed with fear, and a solid ass kicking,

>   Shook the cocky, know-it-all loser

Awakened the divine... Now you decide

>   I love you dad for you are my Blessing in Disguise.

Explanation

"The feelings were impossible to describe, incomprehensible, but through my war with drugs, alcohol, and insanity came a blessing in disguise. He saved me, with a mask of a terrorist, a monster. Thank you."

Also from ThomasMax Publishing
By New Hope Author John Hensel

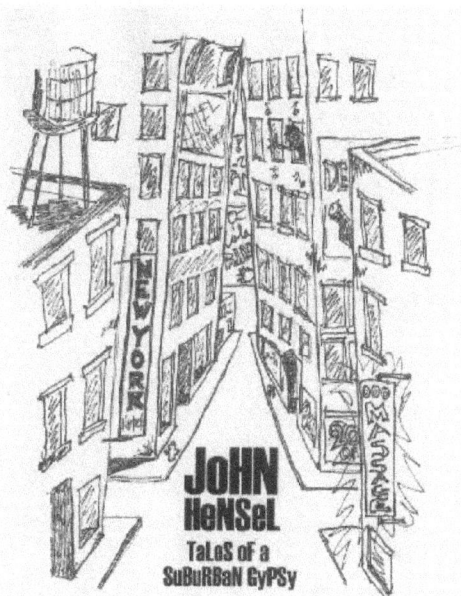

Tales of A Suburban Gypsy, $14.95

New Hope, PA, author John Hensel describes his search for life and love as a Baby Boomer working in music promotion in the era of sex, drugs and rock 'n' roll. Many unusual anecdotes make for a colorful slice of life from decades past.

www.ingramcontent.com/pod-product-compliance
Lightning Source LLC
LaVergne TN
LVHW091200080426
835509LV00006B/768